RIDDLES
FOR
SMART
TEENS

Follow us on social media
to keep up to date with our news,
share what you liked the most and least
and even send us your suggestions!

 /labiblidesados

 @labiblidesados

 @labiblidesados

We've got plenty of other awesome gamebooks designed
just for teens! Scan the QR code if you want to discover
them.

La Bibli des Ados

amazon.us

amazon.co.uk

Table of contents

Tip :
If the puzzle seems too complicated, there must be a simple solution.

Puzzle 1

You participate in your school running race.
It's your lucky day and you overtake the second runner.
What's your new rank ?

Puzzle 2

How can you possibly stay awake for 10 days without sleeping ?

Puzzle 3

The pizza delivery guy is going the wrong way on a one-way street.
There are 3 policemen but none of them arrest him.
Why ?

Puzzle 4

What has 13 hearts, but no stomach nor brain ?

Answers p.66

Puzzle 5

2 fathers and 2 sons are in a camper, yet there are only 3 people in the camper.
Why ?

Puzzle 6

After a breakup, a sad man spends the whole day filling up glasses with alcohol.
Yet, at the end of the day, he is not drunk.
Why ?

Puzzle 7

A dog was outside in the garden when it started to rain heavily. With no place to hide, the poor dog got completely soaked in the rain.
However, its hair isn't wet. Why ?

Puzzle 8

You're in a dark room with a box of matches.
There is a candle, a barbecue lighter and a log. What do you light first?

Answers p.66

Puzzle 9

Trees are my home. However I never get inside them, and if I happen to fall off a tree, I'm certainly dead.
Who am I ?

Puzzle 10

You play chess with your best friend.
You both win.
How is this possible ?

Puzzle 11

It's got 4 fingers and one thumb but it is not alive.
What is that ?

Puzzle 12

What keeps increasing and can never decrease?

Answers p.66

Puzzle 13

What can go through a window without ever breaking it?

Puzzle 14

What goes up to let us go and goes down to make us stay?

Puzzle 15

Here is a list of sports: Rugby, Tennis, Fencing, Football.
Which comes next?
Badminton, Boxing or Basketball?

Puzzle 16

What question can you never theoretically answer "Yes" to?

Answers p.66

Puzzle 17

An electric train makes the Houston > San Antonio route and the wind is blowing from the north.
Which direction is the smoke going?

Puzzle 18

There is a green house. Inside of it, there's a white house, which itself contains a red house. Inside the red house, there are lots of babies. What is that ?

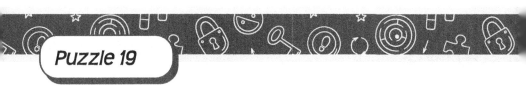

Puzzle 19

Alcohol makes me furious and grow bigger but water can kill me.
What am I ?

Puzzle 20

Which month of the year do people sleep the least?

Answers p.66

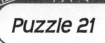

Puzzle 21

What is made of water but dies when you put it in water?

Puzzle 22

I'm big while I'm young and I shrink until I disappear as I get older.
What am I ?

Puzzle 23

I can be thrown from the top of the Eiffel Tower without suffering any damage. On the other hand, if you throw me in a puddle of water, I die. What am I ?

Puzzle 24

The person making it doesn't need it. Whoever buys it has no use for it either. Whoever uses it will not be able to see it or feel it.
What is it ?

Answers p.66

Puzzle 25

5 brothers are busy. Oliver is cooking, Martin is playing chess, Tom is listening to music and Charlie is on the phone. What is the fifth brother doing?

Puzzle 26

A 16-year-old boy celebrated his own birthday only 4 times in his entire life. How is it possible ?

Puzzle 27

What is filled with holes but still manages to retain water?

Puzzle 28

Quote 3 consecutive days without mentioning the days of the week.

Answers p.66

Puzzle 29

3 psychologists say David is their brother.
David says he has no brothers.
Who is lying?

Puzzle 30

A criminal is sentenced to death. He has to choose between 3 rooms: the first one is on fire, the second one is filled up with water and electricity and in the third one there are lions, which haven't been eating for months. Which room is the safest?

Puzzle 31

Mr and Mrs Smith have 5 children.
Half of them are boys.
How is it possible ?

Puzzle 32

What's next ? MTWTFS

Answers p. 66-67

Puzzle 33

Two pieces of wood, a carrot and a scarf lie on the ground in the garden. Nobody put them on the ground but there's a logical explanation they're there.
What is the reason?

Puzzle 34

A man walks into a bar and asks for a glass of water. The bartender pulls out a gun and points it at the man. The man thanks him and leaves.
Why ? What happened ?

Puzzle 35

A child living in a 24-floors burning building decides to jump out of the window.
He manages to escape without any injuries.
How is it possible ?

Puzzle 36

What travels the world but always stays in the same place?

Answers p.67

Puzzle 37

You can hear me, but not see me. I only talk if you talk.
What am I ?

Puzzle 38

When do you go when it's red and stop at green?

Puzzle 39

You will always find me on Mars, Mercury and Jupiter but never on Venus.
What am I ?

Puzzle 40

A group of 4 friends are walking with their dogs. They only have got one umbrella for themselves and their dogs. Surprisingly, no one gets wet.
How is it possible ?

Answers p.67

Puzzle 41

What starts with an "E" and has only one letter inside of it?

Puzzle 42

The day before yesterday, Kyle was 15 years old. Next year he will be 18 years old.
How is it possible ?

Puzzle 43

What lengthens and shortens at the same time?

Puzzle 44

What is bigger than the Giza pyramid but infinitely lighter?

Answers p.67

Puzzle 45

I'm black until I'm used. Then I become red, before ending my life all white.
What am I ?

Puzzle 46

The more guards I have, the less I feel safe.
The fewer guards I have, the more I feel protected.
What am I ?

Puzzle 47

2 sisters were born on the same day of the same year and have the same father and mother.
However, they are not twins.
How is it possible ?

Puzzle 48

What gets sharper the more you use it?

Answers p.67

Puzzle 49

What is yours but also something other people use more than you?

Puzzle 50

Throughout his all career, a doctor treated several thousand patients. But none of them thanked him. Why ?

Puzzle 51

I have a lock but no door. What am I then?

Puzzle 52

When I'm clean I'm black.
When I'm dirty I'm white.
What am I ?

Answers p.67

Puzzle 53

Emily is mute, blind and deaf.
How many senses does she have left?

Puzzle 54

For me, All Saints Day is before Easter and Halloween is after Christmas (in the same year).
What am I?

Puzzle 55

I'm not human but people can't go anywhere without me. I also have 2 legs but I can't walk alone.
What am I?

Puzzle 56

Complete the sequence: 3 - 7 - 8 - 50 - ?

Answers p.67

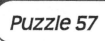

Puzzle 57

If Peter's son is my son's father, who am I to Peter?

Puzzle 58

What can go up a chimney when closed, but cannot go down a chimney when it's open?

Puzzle 59

What is in front of you and yet you cannot see it?

Puzzle 60

I am surrounded by hair and I am in the middle of it. I have an opening that you can see open and closed. What am I?

Answers p.67-68

Puzzle 61

How many animals do I have at home knowing that all but two are dogs, all but two are cats, and all but two are chickens?

Puzzle 62

I put my teeth between your teeth.
Who am I ?

Puzzle 63

A blind man is alone on a desert island. He has 4 pills with him: two blue and two green. His doctor told him to take a blue and a green pill if he wants to live, but not 2 of the same color. How can he do it?

Puzzle 64

I never ask questions but I wait for an answer.
What am I ?

Answers p.68

Puzzle 65

A woman drops her ring into her cup of coffee. She eventually manages to get it back without getting her fingers wet and without spilling the coffee. How does she do it?

Puzzle 66

Before having it, you don't want it.
But once you have it, you don't want to lose it.
What is it ?

Puzzle 67

What is taller sitting than standing?

Puzzle 68

I am dressed in hair.
I am endowed with flesh.
I can produce milk, yet I am not an animal. What am I ?

Answers p.68

Puzzle 69

A man is dead.
Investigators have found the culprit.
However, he will never go to jail.
Why?

Puzzle 70

What animal can jump higher than a building?

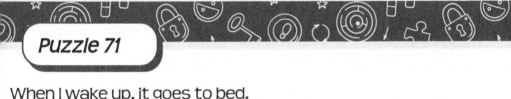

Puzzle 71

When I wake up, it goes to bed.
When I go to bed, it gets up.
What is it ?

Puzzle 72

Which animal has the most teeth?

Answers p.68

Puzzle 73

It only takes one word to separate them.
What is it ?

Puzzle 74

It snowed the day before. A man looks at his neighbour's property and notices that there's twice as much snow as what's on his own property. Why isn't he surprised?

Puzzle 75

What is the intruder and why?
Avocado, Broccoli, Cherry, Radish, Eggplant.

Puzzle 76

When my two parts come together, I separate.
What am I ?

Answers p.68

Puzzle 77

What is the coded message in the calculation: 101x5?

Puzzle 78

What's in the middle of Tokyo?

Puzzle 79

I live in a tongue palate.
I may wear a crown and yet I am neither a queen nor a king.
Who am I ?

Puzzle 80

Find the errror: 1+2 = 3 and 3+5 = 8

Answers p.68

A woman was found dead in her car. The suspects are Alexia, Manon and Eva. There is a calendar in the glove compartment with the numbers 3, 4, 11, 10, 11 written in blood. Who is the culprit?

It's 9:30 p.m. when Julia and Oriana decide to go out for a drink together at a new bar.

They order the same drink.

Oriana was really thirsty and finished five drinks in the time it took Julia to finish one.

The drinks were poisoned, but only Julia died.

What is the explanation for this?

Answers p.68

A woman's corpse lies at the bottom of a multi-floor Parisian building.

It seems that she committed suicide by jumping out of the window.

When the detective arrives, he goes up the first floor of the building, opens the closed window and throws a coin towards the ground. He goes to the second floor and does the exact same thing. He keeps doing this until he gets to the top floor of the building.

When he comes back down, he claims it was murder, not suicide.

How did he find out?

Juliette is at her mother's funeral. There she meets a nice boy and they both get along so well that Juliette ends up having a crush on him.

She was busy at the funeral and didn't have time to ask for his phone number before he left.

She really tried to find him, but no one knew who he was or how to contact him.

A few days later, Juliette's sister dies and the police suspects it to be a murder.

Who killed her sister ?

Answers p.68-69

Lucie went to the police to report that someone had stolen her golden locket.

When the police arrived at her house, they noticed that the window was broken, the interior was a total mess and there were footprints on the floor.

But there were no other signs of a break-in.

A few hours later, the police arrested Lucie for fraud, without having a doubt.

Why ?

A serial killer has kidnapped four different people and made them sit with two pills in their hands and a glass of water.

He tells them to take a pill each, but warns them that one is poisonous and the other harmless.

The killer confidently says:

"I'll take the pill you didn't choose"

All of the victims chose the poisonous pill and died.

How did the serial killer get them to take the poisonous pill?

Answers p.69

A newlywed American couple fly to the Bahamas for their honeymoon.

The husband returns home alone following a horrible accident during a boat excursion.

The local police in charge of the investigation decides to contact the travel agency the couple used to book the trip. Soon after, the police becomes certain the husband is guilty of his wife's murder.

How can they be sure?

Puzzle 88

A chemist was murdered in his own laboratory.

The only evidence was a piece of paper on which the names of chemical elements were written.

These substances were Bromine, Uranium and Nobelium.

The chemist only saw 4 people passing through his laboratory on the day of the murder: his friend William, his wife Celia, his intern Bruno and his colleague Ethan.

The police immediately arrested the murderer.

How did they know who it was?

Réponses p.69

In a motel in a remote village in Cleveland, a cleaning lady is alerted by a gunshot.

She immediately decides to call the police.

They discover a corpse lying in a pool of blood, a smartphone in one hand and a gun in the other.

You could listen to a recording of a few seconds on the phone: "I can't go on like this, my life no longer has any meaning" followed by a gunshot.

The police thinks it is a murder and not a suicide.

What made them realized that?

Every day at a toll booth on the Franco-Spanish border, customs officers see a woman crossing the border carrying sandbags on a motorbike.

After a while, the customs officers decide to arrest her, only to find that she only has sand on her and let her go.

What is this woman smuggling into France?

Answers p.69

A duke from a wealthy family has no wife or children.
He is near the end of his life and he would like to find an
heir to bequeath all his property and fortune.
He gives every child in the village a seed and says that
whoever grows the biggest and most beautiful plant will
inherit his fortune.
When the day comes, all children show him gargantuan
plants, but he ends up choosing a little girl with an empty
flowerpot as his heir. Why ?

In a chic hotel located in the 16th arrondissement of Paris, a
woman opens the door of her room to a man who has just
knocked.
The man immediately apologizes saying that he thought it
was his own room.
Immediately after leaving, the woman grabs her phone and
calls the police.
Why ?

Answers p.69

Puzzle 93

We are in a small country village with a hill overlooking the village.

This village's peculiarity is that all the inhabitants can see a huge tower located at the very top of the hill.

A serial killer who gives clues in advance about each of his crimes leaves the following clue:

"Tonight I will kill someone in the only place in the village where it is impossible to observe the tower".

How did the investigators finally manage to catch him?

Puzzle 94

In a village in East Texas a lawyer is found dead in his office.

He was lying in a pool of blood, his head on his desk next to a pistol and a pen in his hand.

The powder found in his ear indicated that the blow had been given at close range, suggesting a suicide.

In addition, a letter was placed on the desk where the lawyer expressed the reasons for his suicide.

However, the sheriff in charge of the case thinks it's a murder.

Why ?

Answers p.69

After being in a coma for 27 days, Margaret died on September 12 2021, at the age of 83. The news saddened his son Jacob but he was mostly surprised by the announcement of his uncle Henri: "I will inherit all my sister's fortune".
Margaret wrote a will 4 years before and she showed it to Jacob. It stated that after her death, his son would inherit 90% of her fortune and his uncle Harry would get the rest. Jacob examined a copy of the new will that Harry had presented to him. It dated back to August 31 2021, and stated that Henri would inherite all the fortune. It had the signature of Margaret and 2 witnesses. Jacob is sure it's a fake.
Why ?

Robin is locked up in a prison cell with the shape of a 13 foot cube. The walls are made of reinforced concrete and the foundations go 10 feet underground.
The only openings are an armored door locked with 3 locks and a ceiling opening with a 3 foot diameter.
Robin believes he has found a way to escape and therefore he begins digging a tunnel.
He knows he won't be able to get out using the tunnel, but it's part of his plan.
How does he plan to escape?

Answers p.69

A macabre evening of December 24 in Chicago...
A woman had been shot on her way to her family's house for Christmas dinner.
Her body lay next to her car in the snowy driveway that leads to her family's house.
Footprints between two parallel tire tracks led to the victim.
What type of individual should the investigator look for in order to solve this case?

A wealthy retired woman spends the end of her life alone in a remote English country mansion.
As she can no longer move, she has her shopping and everything else she needs delivered at her house.
On a Friday, the paperboy realizes something is wrong when he sees the windows open in the freezing cold. He decides to enter and sees the lifeless body of the retiree.
Around her body, there's the Tuesday paper, a sewing catalog and some cookies. The medical examiner estimates time of death dating back at least 48 hours.
Who should the inspector suspect and why?

Answers p.70

Police have been searching for a man in the mountains, after one of his relatives reported him as missing.
A police team manages to locate his position from their helicopter after several hours of research.
They find the poor man's lifeless body in the snow.
No footprints were visible and his death was due partially to his backpack, which remained closed.
He didn't die of thirst, hunger or cold.
What is in the victim's backpack that could have caused his death?

An investigator asks his informant for information concerning an arms trafficker well known to his agency:
"Do you know where he is currently hiding?"
The informant answers he does and that he can even tell him precisely where to find him:
"According to my sources, he is hiding in 3 houses located side by side. I can even give you the numbers: 24, 25 and 26 Olvera street."
The investigator immediately understands that he can no longer trust his informant.
Why ?

Answers p.70

Puzzle 101

Divide the number 110 into two parts so that one gives 50% more than the other. What are the two numbers?

Puzzle 102

Find the 3 positive numbers that give 6 when multiplied or added together.

Puzzle 103

On a bus there are a 28-year-old pregnant woman, a 71-year-old retired man, a conductor who is twice the age of the pregnant woman and a 54-year-old businessman. Who is the youngest?

Puzzle 104

Which figure or number divided by itself gives its double as a result?

Answers p.70

Puzzle 105

A slug is in a 12-meter-deep well. It climbs 3 meters every day and falls back down 2 meters every night. In how many days will it reach the top of the well?

Puzzle 106

1=5
2=25
3=325
4=4325
5=?

Puzzle 107

Aaron is 8 years old.
His little brother Lucas is half his age.
When Aaron is 10 times older, how old will Lucas be?

Puzzle 108

At a farm, there are 3 rabbits, 4 cows, 12 people, 6 ducks and 2 dogs.
How many paws are there?

Answers p.70

Puzzle 109

I am 4 times my daughter's age.
In 20 years, I will be twice her age.
How old are we?

Puzzle 110

I am a 3 digit number.
My second digit is 4 times bigger than my first one.
You can multiply my third digit by 7 to find the first 2 digits.
What is the number ?

Puzzle 111

4 hens are able to lay a total of 4 eggs every 4 minutes.
How many hens does it take to have 200 eggs in 200 minutes?

Puzzle 112

By using 8 times the number 8 in an addition (and only this number), we can get the number 1000.
What is the addition to be made?

Answers p.70

Puzzle 113

What mathematical symbol must be added- and where- to the number 66666 to end up with 600 as a result of the calculation?

Puzzle 114

A new and not very orderly delivery man delivers parcels in a building. It starts with the third floor, goes up 4 floors, down 2 floors, up 7 floors and up another floor.
What floor is he on at the end of his tour?

Puzzle 115

Jake the squirrel eats a nut on Monday, 2 on Tuesday, 4 on Wednesday and so on...
How many hazelnuts does he eat per week?

Puzzle 116

If Seth and his little brother Alex step on a scale, it displays 28kg.
Knowing that Seth is 3 times the weight of his little brother, how much does Alex weigh?

Answers P.70

Puzzle 117

If you were born in an odd year, will you turn 18 in an odd or even year?

Puzzle 118

4 friends take part in a marathon. Nathalie finishes 3 minutes ahead of Sandy and Julie finishes 6 minutes ahead of Helena. Helena needed 4 minutes more than Nathalie to finish. In what order did they arrive?

Puzzle 119

128 tennis players are involved in a knockout tournament. How many matches will the winner need to win the tournament?

Puzzle 120

A bricklayer carries an 18-kilo bag of cement. He removes half of the cement but notices that the bag weighs 10 kilos. What is the weight of the empty bag?

Answers p.70-71

Puzzle 121

I add 5 to 21 and I get 2.
The answer is correct, but how is it possible?

Puzzle 122

A south France breeder has 100 pairs of cows in his paddock.
If 2 pairs of calves are born per cow and 83 of them die at birth, how many animals are left in total?

Puzzle 123

A small clothing store retailer sets his prices in a peculiar way. Socks cost $5, jackets $7 and hats $4. Using this method, how much would the sweaters cost?

Puzzle 124

Kevin wrote all the numbers from 200 to 300 on a paper.
How many times did he write the number 2?

Answers p.71

Puzzle 125

How many days are there in 4 years time ?

Puzzle 126

A pumpkin and a candle cost $1.10.
The pumpkin costs $1 more than the candle.
How much does the candle cost?

Puzzle 127

Alexa is 54 years old and her father John is 80 years old.
How many years back in time John was 3 times the age of his daughter?

Puzzle 128

If it were two hours later, there would be half as much time left before midnight as if it were one hour later. What time is it right now ?

Answers p.71

You have to use the figure 9 four times (and only this figure) to get the number 100.
How do you do?

Puzzle 130

A snail is 10 meters away from a house. Every day it advances half the distance that separates it from the house. In how many days will it reach the house?

Puzzle 131

Your friends contributed all together to get you a nice present. At first, 10 friends participated but 2 dropped out. The 8 others had to add 10$ more to obtain the initial amount. How much money does the gift cost?

Puzzle 132

Several photos are lined up on a wall.
If a photo is 6th from the left and 8th from the right, how many photos are there in the row?

Answers p.71

Puzzle 133

Arnaud was 5 years old when he drove a nail into a tree in his grandparents' garden to mark his height. He returned there at the age of 15. Knowing that the tree grew 2 inches each year, how much higher would the nail be?

Puzzle 134

My aunt's house number is the opposite of mine (ex: 24 and 42). The difference between our house numbers ends with the number 2. What are the lowest possible numbers of our houses?

Puzzle 135

Karen says of her little sister Jennifer: "2 years ago, I was 3 times her age. In 3 years, I will be twice her age."
How old are the two sisters?

Puzzle 136

If 7 basketball players meet and only shake hands once before playing, how many handshakes will there be?

Answers p.71

How can you make this operation correct without changing it?

8 + 8 = 91

A bodybuilding club has 300 members. 5% of them have a tattoo. Of the remaining 95%, half has 2 tattoos and the other half has none.
What is the total number of tattoos?

Find the missing digit:
1=3, 2=3, 3=5, 4=4, 5= ?

What symbols are missing to make the equation correct?

8 4 8 4 = 36

Answers p.71

Puzzle 141

1
11
21
1211
What's next ?

Puzzle 142

Jordan paid €46 with 33 €1 or €2 coins only.
How many €2 coins did he use?

Puzzle 143

Michael blew out a candle at one year, 2 at 2 years, 3 at 3 years...
Today, he will have blown out 153 birthday candles.
How old is Michael?

Puzzle 144

13 people are gathered to celebrate Christmas at the Moore's. Each one gives a gift to the others.
How many gifts are there under the tree?

Answers p.72

Puzzle 145

Max is 5 times older than Tom. 4 years ago, he was 7 times older than him.
How old is Max?

Puzzle 146

Louis controls the number of scooters that enter a parking lot. He saw 20 scooters entering, for a total of 48 wheels. How many 3-wheel scooters came in?

Puzzle 147

The price of a cryptocurrency is 10$ for one unit on Monday. This cryptocurrency price increases by 50% on Tuesday then it drops by 50% on Wednesday. How many dollars is a unit worth on Wednesday?

Puzzle 148

Sam's bag contains 50 marbles of different colors: red, green, blue, yellow, orange, and purple. How many marbles must be drawn at least to be sure to have 2 marbles of the same color?

Answers p.72

Answers p.72

Puzzle 149

3, 6, 4, 12, 9, 36, 32, ...
What is the logical sequence?

Puzzle 150

Marie has all her savings on 3 different accounts, i.e.
$2100. Two-thirds are placed in account A, 20% in account
B and the rest in account C.
How many dollars does she have in account C?

Puzzle 151

3 sisters must share an inheritance of 22,000$. The first
sister receives 1,000$ more than the third one. The second
sister receives $3,000 less than twice what the third sister
got. What share does each sister end up receiving?

Puzzle 152

A gold bar weighs 17 ounces + half a gold bar.
How much does a gold bar weigh?

Answers p.72

Puzzle 153

In a bar, 15 people dance, 13 people have a drink in their hands and 7 people dance with a drink in their hands. 9 people don't dance and don't have a drink.
How many customers are there in the bar (excluding staff)?

Puzzle 154

A little bit careless, Chris forgets to write the comma on his check when paying for his shopping.
That mistake cost him $1,826.55 too much.
What number should Chris have written on the check?

Puzzle 155

In a group of friends, 60% wear a red sweater, 65% wear red pants and 90% wear red shoes. What minimum percentage of boys wear only red clothes?

Puzzle 156

On the way to school, you count 42 houses on your right and on the way back, 42 on your left.
How many houses are there in total?

Answers p.72

Puzzle 157

What number do you get by multiplying all the digits on your smartphone when it is in dialpad mode?

Puzzle 158

John and Nicolas race for 200 meters.
Nicolas wins the 1st race with a 10 meter lead.
For revenge, Nicolas starts 10m behind John to balance the race out. Who wins the rematch?

Puzzle 159

Dustin places an inflatable buoy on his swimming pool.
What will cause the water level to rise the most?
Throwing a €2 coin in the water or on the buoy?

Puzzle 160

If the weight of a number is equal to the sum of its digits, which smaller number will weigh the number 20?

Answers p.72

Puzzle 161

How many squares are there in this picture?

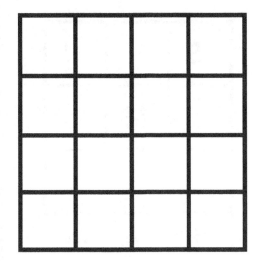

Puzzle 162

How many triangles are there in this picture?

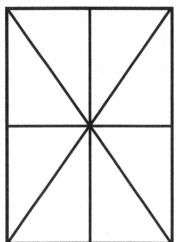

Puzzle 163

How many squares are there in this picture?

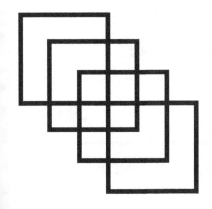

Puzzle 164

How many triangles are there in this picture?

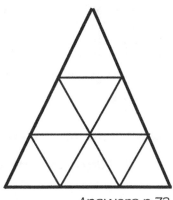

Answers p.73

The magic square game!
Each line (horizontal, vertical and diagonal) must sum
to the same number

9		
		10
		3

The sum must be : 18

15		11
	12	

The sum must be : 36

17		25
22		

The sum must be : 63

38	42	
		39

The sum must be : 126

Answers p.73

Solve the additive pyramids!
Each box must be the sum of the 2 boxes below it.

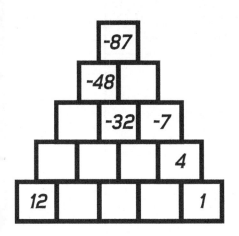

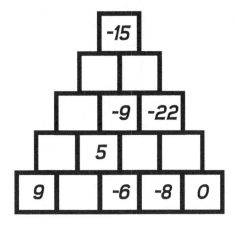

Do the same with the multiplicative pyramids!

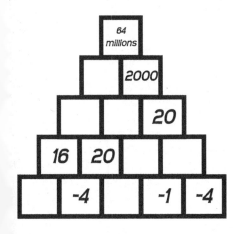

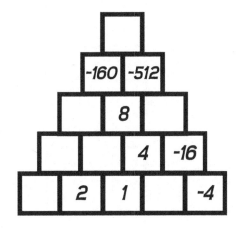

Answers p.73

Difficulty :

8	3					5		
7						8	2	4
	1				4		6	
	8	9	2	6			5	
	2			5	8	1	3	
	4		1				7	
9	6	2						5
		8					4	9

Difficulty :

5	4	2			1	9	7	
					5	2		
		3	9					
2	9					5	4	6
7	8	4					1	2
					9	1		
		6	1					
	7	9	8			4	3	5

Answers p.73

Difficulty :

	1	5					3	
				4		1		
3		7	1				8	2
		3			2			8
4	7						1	5
9			5			4		
5	6				3	8		9
		8		9				
	9					3	7	

Difficulty :

		1	2	9		6	3	
		7	6		8		2	
		2			4			5
	5							3
		6				9		
8							4	
6			4			3		
	9		7		1	2		
	2	5		6	3	4		

Answers p.74

Puzzle 177

Puzzle 178

 Find out the secret code!

The sum of the 4 digits is 13, the thousands digit is 2 times greater than the units digit and the hundreds digit is 3 times greater than the tens digit:

The sum of the 4 digits is 18, the thousands digit is 3 times smaller than the units digit and the hundreds digit is equal to the tens digit:

Puzzle 179

Puzzle 180

The sum of the 4 digits is 20 and the hundreds digit is the same as the units digit. The thousands digit is one quarter of the sum of the hundreds and ones.
The tens digit is the same as the thousands digit.

The sum of the 4 digits is 27. The units digit is equal to the sum of thousands and hundreds -1. The tens digit is equal to the units digit -1. The thousands digit is 5.

Answers p.74

Quiz 181

Theme: sports

How did the 2018 FIFA World Cup final between France and Croatia end?

A) 2 - 1
B) 2 - 2
C) 3 - 2
D) 4 - 2

Quiz 182

Theme: sports

The Olympic games take place...

A) Every year
B) Every 2 years
C) Every 4 years
D) Every 5 years

Answers p.74

Quiz 183

Theme: sports

Who won the NBA championship in 2021?

A) Los Angeles Lakers
B) Milwaukee Bucks
C) Toronto Raptors
D) Golden State Warriors

Quiz 184

Theme: sports

In which sport can you make a "spare"?

A) Billiards
B) Curling
C) Darts
D) Bowling

Answers p.74

Quiz 185

Theme: *History & Geography*

Apartheid was a policy that aimed to separate people based on their skin color.
Where was it set up?

A) In Algeria
B) In South Africa
C) In Australia
D) In France

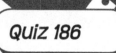

Quiz 186

Theme: *History & Geography*

On what date did the United Kingdom leave the European Union (also know as "the Brexit")?

A) December 31, 2019
B) January 31, 2020
C) June 30, 2020
D) January 31, 2021

Answers p.74

Theme: *History & Geography*

In which country is Kilimanjaro, the highest mountain in Africa, located?

A) In Tanzania
B) In Kenya
C) In Cameroon
D) In Somalia

Theme: *History & Geography*

Which country's flag is a blue cross on a white background?

A) Finland
B) Sweden
C) Norway
D) Iceland

Answers p.74

Theme: Music

How many strings does an electric guitar usually have?

A) 5
B) 6
C) 7
D) 8

Theme: Music

Which instrument bears the name of its inventor?

A) The saxophone
B) The violin
C) The piano
D) The harp

Answers p.74

Theme: Music

Which of the following instruments is not a string instrument?

A) The piano
B) The guitar
C) The double bass
D) The marimba

Theme: Music

What is a tablature?

A) A music stand used by conductors
B) A form of music sheet mostly used by guitarists
C) An element of an organ
D) A medieval instrument

Answers p.74

Theme: Cinema

In which city does the Oscar ceremony take place?

A) Los Angeles
B) London
C) Seattle
D) New-York

Quiz 194

Theme: Cinema

Which country produces the most films?

A) The United States
B) India
C) France
D) Russia

Answers p.75

Quiz 195

Theme: Cinema

What is the director's role in a film?

A) He is the one who direct the production of the film
B) He finances the film
C) He takes care of the sound recording
D) He films actors and actresses

Quiz 196

Theme: Cinema

Who invented motion pictures ?

A) Lucien Eiffel
B) Thomas Edison
C) The Lumière brothers
D) Nikola Tesla

Answers p.75

Quiz 197

Theme: Animals

Which animal cannot fly ?

A) The auk
B) The penguin
C) The crane
D) The stork

Quiz 198

Theme: Animals

What animal bellows?

A) The deer
B) The wolf
C) The beaver
D) The elephant

Answers p.75

Theme: Animals

How many years ago did the dinosaurs go extinct?

A) 50 million
B) 55 million
C) 60 million
D) 65 million

Theme: Animals

Which animal is the fastest?

A) The jaguar
B) The cheetah
C) The gazelle
D) The hare

Answers p.75

SSSSSSS

OOOOOOO

LLLLLLL

UUUUUUU

TTTTTTT

I I I I I I I

OOOOOOO

NNNNNNN

SSSSSSS

1. Second place
2. While sleeping at night
3. Because he is on foot
4. A card game
5. They're the grandfather, the father and the son
6. He is a bartender
7. The dog has no hair
8. A match
9. Leaf
10. Both of you are playing against another team (chess can be played 2v2)
11. A glove
12. Your age
13. The light
14. An anchor
15. Badminton (in the list, each sport has one more letter than the previous sport)
16. "Do you sleep ?"
17. An electric train does not produce smoke
18. A watermelon
19. Fire
20. February (because there are fewer days)
21. Ice cube
22. A candle
23. A piece of paper
24. A coffin
25. He's playing chess
26. He was born on February 29
27. A sponge
28. Yesterday, today and tomorrow
29. No one, David has 3 psychologist sisters.
30. The one with the lions because they died.

31. The other half are also boys.

32. S (Sunday)

33. They were used by kids who made a snowman. The snow has since melted

34. The man was hiccuping and the bartender understood it while he asked for a glass of water. So he scared him to help the man get rid of the hiccups.

35. He lives on the first floor of this building

36. A stamp

37. The echo

38. When you eat a watermelon

39. The Letter R

40. It wasn't raining

41. An envelope

42. Yesterday was December 31, Kyle turned 16. This year he will be 17 and next year 18.

43. Life

44. His shadow

45. Charcoal

46. A secret

47. They have a third sister and are therefore triplets

48. A brain

49. Your first name

50. Because he's a veterinarian

51. A padlock

52. A chalkboard

53. 3: touch, taste and smell.

54. A dictionary

55. Pants

56. 60! When written, all numbers have 5 letters.

57. Son-in-law (step-son)

58. An umbrella

59. The future

60. An eye

61. A dog, a cat and a hen

62. A fork

63. He eats half of each pill

64. Your Phone

65. She drinks her coffee while the ring is still in it

66. War

67. A dog

68. Coconut

69. The man committed suicide

70. None because a building cannot jump

71. My foot

72. The Tooth Fairy

73. Lips

74. The neighbor's garden is twice bigger

75. Radish (this is the only one that does not follow the alphabetical order)

76. Scissors

77. SOS because 101x5 = 505

78. The letter "K"

79. A Tooth

80. There are 3 "R"s to error.

81. Manon is the culprit. The numbers represent the first letter of each month (3 = March, 4 = April, 11 = November, 10 = October, 11 = November)

82. The ice cubes were poisoned. They didn't have time to melt into Oriana's glass as she drank rapidly.

83. He knows this because all the windows on each floor were closed and therefore she could not have committed suicide.

84. She herself killed her sister in the hope of seeing the boy again at her funeral.

85. The police immediately understood that Lucie was the cause of the broken window because the pieces of glass were on the outside. Which means she's the one who broke the window from the inside.

86. None of the pills were poisoned, only the water in the victims' glasses was.

87. The husband had booked a return flight only for him.

88. The clue is on the piece of paper! The symbols of the chemical elements are Br, U, No: BRUNO.

89. Remember, the recording only lasted a few seconds. If it were a suicide, the phone would still be recording. The killer made the mistake of stopping it.

90. Motorcycles of course!

91. The Duke only distributed fake seeds that had no chance of growing. The little girl was the only one who didn't cheat.

92. Because if he really thought it was his room, he wouldn't have knocked on the door.

93. Investigators understood that the killer would commit his crime inside the tower.

94. If it really was a suicide, the lawyer would not have had the pen in his hand, but rather the gun.

95. Margaret had been in a coma for 27 days, so she could not have written a will on August 31 2021, 12 days before her death.

96. Robin intends to use the soil he will accumulate while digging, to climb on it and escape through the opening in the ceiling.

97. A person in a wheelchair! The footprints are certainly belongs to the victim and the wheel tracks are those of a wheelchair.

98. The newspaper boy, since he was aware of her death, as he didn't deliver the Wednesday and Thursday newspapers.

99. The victim jumped from an airplane but his parachute did not open.

100. Houses with even numbers are never on the same side of the street as the ones with odd numbers.

101. 66+44

102. 1, 2 and 3 (1 + 2 + 3 = 6 and 1 x 2 x 3 = 6)

103. The baby

104. 0.5 (0.5: 0.5 = 1)

105. In 10 days! The slug climbs 1 meter each day (3 - 2). It finds itself at 9 meters on the 9th day. It will therefore be at 12 meters (out of the well) on the 10th day.

106. 5 = 1

107. 76 years old (80 - 4)

108. 48 (people have no paws)

109. I am 40 years old and my daughter is 10 years old

110. 284

111. 2 hens (they lay at a frequency of 1 egg per minute)

112. 888 + 88 + 8 + 8 + 8 = 1000

113. 666 - 66 = 600

114. On the 13th floor

115. 127 hazelnuts

116. 7 pounds

117. Odd

118. Julie, Nathalie, Sandy, Helena

119. 7 games (64th, 32nd, 16th, 8th, quarter-final, semi-final and final)

120. 2 kilos

121. If you add 5 a.m. to 9 p.m., it's 2 a.m.

122. 917! 100 x 2 = 200, 200 + 800 = 1000, 1000 - 83 = 917

123. 5$ (each letter costs 1$)

124. 120 times

125. 1461. (4x365) + 1 = 1461 (we add 1 because there is a leap year every 4 years)

126. The candle costs 5 cents. The pumpkin costs 1$ more than the candle, so 1.05$. The total is 1.05$ + 0.05$ = 1.10$.

127. 41 years ago.

128. 9 p.m.

129. 99 + 9:9 = 100

130. It will never be able to reach the house.

131. 400$ (10x40$ or 8x50$)

132. 13

133. The nail is always in the same place as a tree grows to the top.

134. 19 and 91

135. 17 and 7 years old

136. 21 (not 42)

137. Flipping the book upside down! (8+8 = 16)

138. 300! According to our information, 5% or 15 of them have only one tattoo. Among the remaining 95%, or 285 members, half of them has two tattoos and the other half has none. This is the equivalent of saying that all members have a tattoo.

139. 5=4 (the answer represents the number of letters in each digit)

140. 8x (4:8 + 4) = 36

141. 111221 (you must read the previous sequence of numbers aloud to figure out the next line of numbers)

142. 13

143. 17 years old

144. (12x13 = 156)

145. Max is 60 years old

146. Louis having seen 20 scooters coming in, he should have seen 40 wheels. However, he counted 48 or 8 more. So there were 8 scooters with 3 wheels and 12 with 2 wheels.

147. $7.5 (if the currency increases by 50% on Tuesday, it then goes to $15. Losing 50% on Wednesday, it drops to $7.5)

148.7

149. 160 (multiply by 2 and subtract 2, then multiply by 3 and subtract 3 and so on...)

150. 280$ (2100 - 1400 - 420 = 280)

151. Sister 1: 7000$, Sister 2: 9000$, Sister 3: 6000$

152. 34 ounces

153. 30 customers (8+6+7+9)

154. $18.45. As Chris forgot the comma, this means he paid 100 times the price for his shopping. That is 99 more. You therefore calculate 1826.55: 99 = 18.45

155. 15% (40% don't have a red sweater, 35% don't have red pants, and 10% don't have red shoes.
40+35+10 = 85% are not completely dressed in red)

156. 42! These are the same houses on the way there and back.

157. 0 (we must not forget the number 0. Any number multiplied by zero is zero.)

158. Nicolas (He runs 200m while John runs 190. On the 2nd race, Nicolas (starting 10m behind) reaches 190m at the same time as John. Since there are 10m left and being Nicolas faster than John, he wins again).

159. On the buoy (in the water, the coin displaces its water volume, while on the buoy the coin displaces its water weight).

160. 199kg (1+9+9=20)

161. 30

162. 16

163. 15

164. 13

165.
9	4	5
2	6	10
7	8	3

166.
15	10	11
8	12	16
13	14	9

167.
24	19	20
17	21	25
22	23	18

168.
45	40	41
38	42	46
43	44	39

169.

```
              -87
          -48     -39
      -16     -32     -7
    5     -21     -11     4
  12    -7    -14     3     1
```

170.

```
             -15
          16     -31
       25     -9     -22
    20     5     -14     -8
   9    11    -6    -8     0
```

171.

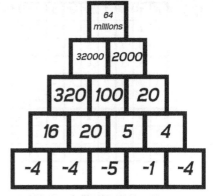

```
                64 millions
            32000       2000
         320      100       20
       16      20       5       4
     -4     -4     -5     -1     -4
```

172.

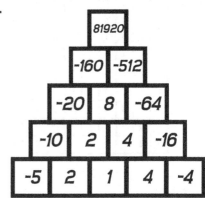

```
              81920
           -160     -512
        -20      8      -64
      -10      2      4      -16
     -5      2      1      4      -4
```

173.
8	3	4	6	7	2	5	9	1
7	9	6	3	1	5	8	2	4
2	1	5	8	9	4	7	6	3
3	8	9	2	6	1	4	5	7
6	5	1	7	4	3	9	8	2
4	2	7	9	5	8	1	3	6
5	4	3	1	2	9	6	7	8
9	6	2	4	8	7	3	1	5
1	7	8	5	3	6	2	4	9

174.
5	4	2	6	8	1	9	7	3
9	6	7	3	4	5	2	8	1
8	1	3	9	2	7	6	5	4
2	9	1	7	3	8	5	4	6
6	3	5	2	1	4	7	9	8
7	8	4	5	9	6	3	1	2
3	2	8	4	5	9	1	6	7
4	5	6	1	7	3	8	2	9
1	7	9	8	6	2	4	3	5

175.

6	1	5	2	8	7	9	3	4
8	2	9	3	4	6	1	5	7
3	4	7	1	5	9	6	8	2
1	5	3	4	6	2	7	9	8
4	7	6	9	3	8	2	1	5
9	8	2	5	7	1	4	6	3
5	6	1	7	2	3	8	4	9
7	3	8	6	9	4	5	2	1
2	9	4	8	1	5	3	7	6

176.

5	8	1	2	9	7	6	3	4
3	4	7	6	5	8	1	2	9
9	6	2	1	3	4	8	7	5
2	5	4	8	1	9	7	6	3
7	3	6	5	4	2	9	1	8
8	1	9	3	7	6	5	4	2
6	7	8	4	2	5	3	9	1
4	9	3	7	8	1	2	5	6
1	2	5	9	6	3	4	8	7

177. 6313

178. 3339

179. 4848

180. 5589

181. 4-2

182. Every 4 years

183. Milwaukee Bucks

184. Bowling

185. In South Africa

186. January 31, 2020

187. In Tanzania

188. Finland

189. 6

190. The saxophone (invented by Mr Sax)

191. The marimba

192. A form of music sheet

193. Los Angeles
194. India
195. He is the one who directs the work production
196. The Lumiere brothers
197. The auk
198. The deer
199. 65 millions
200. The cheetah

Did you like this book?
You can share your thoughts with us by scanning
the QR code below:

amazon.us

amazon.co.uk

Made in the USA
Las Vegas, NV
06 November 2024

11234100R00049